IT'S TIME TO EAT A BABACO

It's Time to Eat a Babaco

Walter the Educator

Silent King Books
A WhichHead Entertainment Imprint

Copyright © 2024 by Walter the Educator

All rights reserved. No part of this book may be reproduced in any manner whatsoever without written per- mission except in the case of brief quotations embodied in critical articles and reviews.

First Printing, 2024

Disclaimer

This book is a literary work; the story is not about specific persons, locations, situations, and/or circumstances unless mentioned in a historical context. Any resemblance to real persons, locations, situations, and/or circumstances is coincidental. This book is for entertainment and informational purposes only. The author and publisher offer this information without warranties expressed or implied. No matter the grounds, neither the author nor the publisher will be accountable for any losses, injuries, or other damages caused by the reader's use of this book. The use of this book acknowledges an understanding and acceptance of this disclaimer.

It's Time to Eat a Babaco is a collectible early learning book by Walter the Educator suitable for all ages belonging to Walter the Educator's Time to Eat Book Series. Collect more books at WaltertheEducator.com

USE THE EXTRA SPACE TO TAKE NOTES AND DOCUMENT YOUR MEMORIES

BABACO

It's time to eat a fruit so sweet,

It's Time to Eat a

Babaco

A Babaco treat, what a tasty feat!

Yellow and bright, smooth to the touch,

Oh, this juicy fruit, we love it so much!

Babaco, Babaco, five sides to see,

Shaped like a star, as fun as can be!

We slice it up with care and grace,

Each piece brings a smile to my face.

It's soft inside, oh what a delight,

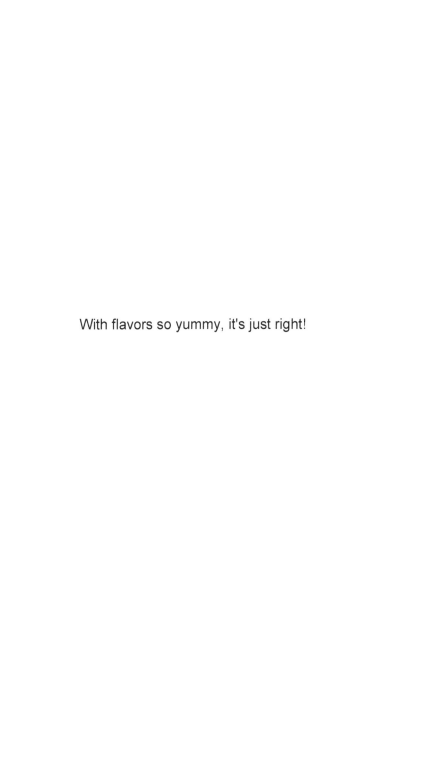
With flavors so yummy, it's just right!

A mix of pineapple, papaya, and pear,

A magical taste floating in the air.

The juice runs down, drips from my chin,

That's how you know the fun will begin!

Take a bite, feel the fruity cheer,

Babaco time is finally here!

It's Time to Eat a

Babaco

No seeds to fuss, just soft and smooth,

With every bite, I start to groove!

It wiggles, it jiggles, so fresh and light,

Eating Babaco makes everything bright.

Let's chew, let's munch, with every crunch,

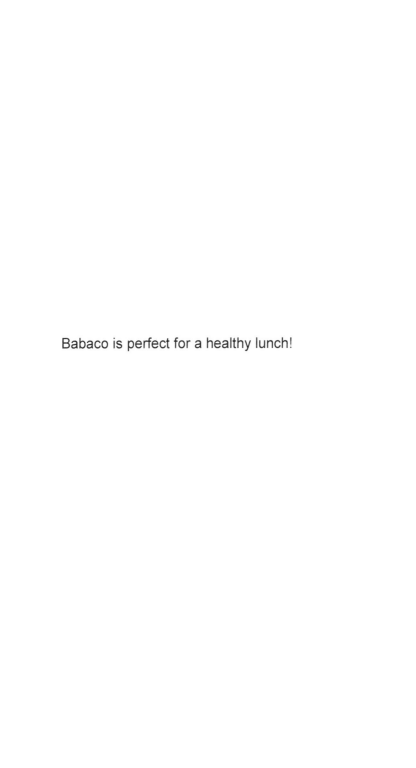

Babaco is perfect for a healthy lunch!

So come along, don't wait too long,

This fruit will make you strong and strong.

Babaco, Babaco, what a treat!

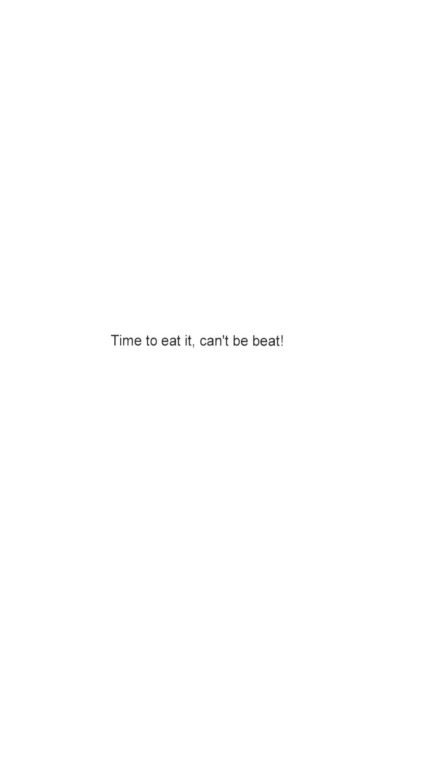

So share with friends, and take a seat,

Babaco fruit is fun to eat!

Babaco fruit, so cool and neat,

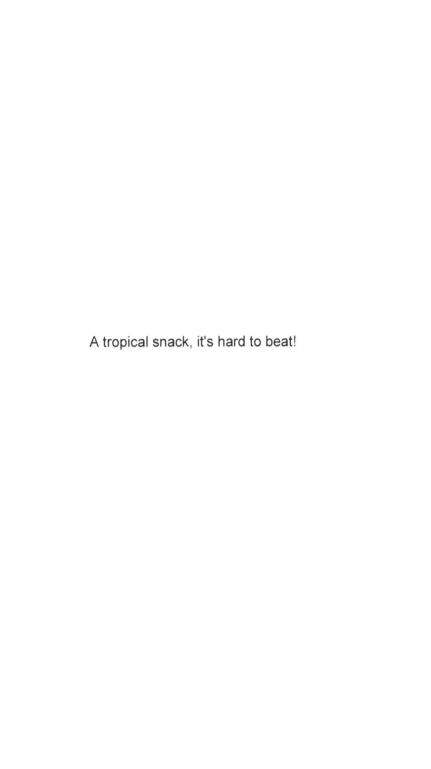

A tropical snack, it's hard to beat!

From Ecuador, it travels far,

Now it's here, our little star.

We wash it clean, slice and share,

Its fruity scent fills up the air.

No need to peel, just eat it whole,

It's Time to Eat a

Babaco

Babaco's here to fill our bowl.

So grab your fork, give it a try,

Babaco's flavors make you sigh!

One more bite, we smile and say,

We'll eat this fruit again someday!

ABOUT THE CREATOR

Walter the Educator is one of the pseudonyms for Walter Anderson. Formally educated in Chemistry, Business, and Education, he is an educator, an author, a diverse entrepreneur, and he is the son of a disabled war veteran. "Walter the Educator" shares his time between educating and creating. He holds interests and owns several creative projects that entertain, enlighten, enhance, and educate, hoping to inspire and motivate you. Follow, find new works, and stay up to date with Walter the Educator™

at WaltertheEducator.com

Milton Keynes UK
Ingram Content Group UK Ltd.
UKHW032038191024
449814UK00011B/652